Love

Songs

KARL HICKEN

Shrubs Publishing

Contents

bliss

note on a queued score, a smear of pigment splashed on parchment, a single utterance on the ears of the impassioned…to touch the ethereal plane. lifting the spirit, immortalizing the secret winds, soaring on an author unknown, only felt in the folds of dreams. this place, this ray of zealous warmth, sought, only to fringe, never to enter fully, reside. to softly rap at the gate, to plead and stretch, strain. i know you, not the person, but the persona, take me with you. and i am taken by you, to become the wings, the breath beneath. the sweet scent of the nocturne sky carrying the trades of the climes pales to you. a quiver, a gentle soul shudder, heights unrivaled, not recognized, known.

this kiss, this love affair of words, the lips

 that utter,

enchantment

euphoria

pleasure

elation

bliss

sent with love

my sweetest friend

o stay with your thoughts and what we shared last night made me teary. this place, this place of zealous warmth, sought, without finding residence is not that of brick and mortar, but of love and acceptance. you are enveloping me in such beauty. looking for you and the persona that you are. take me with you. i am taken by you. it is an invitation to be how i see and always saw you to be. this love, this kiss, this love affair of words, the lips that utter. i don't want to scare you. i need you to know the last thing i want to do is scare you. yes, we have always been in love. it is life and bumps and disappointments and hurtful relationships and events that have found residence where the innocence of who we were and maybe who we are. My sweetest friend, journey 35 has found has offered ownership to you. it was written for you in a time when love was make believe and empty. 35 has beauty, it is tender, is it you? i have penned for you. i am not for looking for your commitment, contrary, love would never do that. i can't remember 48 hours that have thrilled my soul. thank you. where this goes, WOW, there is truth and better still i know i love you.

love you more

sweetest debbie,

softly indulgent, symphonies of thought, brushed with velvet strokes onto the canvas of the soul. immersed in the solitude of a resounding score, each note a shiver, each strain an echo undulating. billowing, swelling, bursting onto a floodplain of desire, each parched sensory receptor melting into the richness. basking in the glow of the authors very image, inspiration melds into tapestry. to pen the mellifluous aspirations captivates this medium of expression. these modest words, so inadequate, pay mere perfunctory veneration, without exquisite instrumentation. howbeit may this humble verse with design to mesmerize and inspire, ignite the fiery blaze of passion, gently impart, and finally seduce. It tickles me to send you slivers of me. to write to you my heart races and my hands shake with what you have done to me. i love it! i love this! i hope you feel the same.

love you more

sweetest deb

i am no super hero. i had a burning need to put myself out there publicly, which has been extraordinarily interesting. i had a wife who wanted nothing to do with it except when someone told her one of my journeys was to solicit the services of a prostitute. i think no prostitute would want to take me even to a scurvy diner no matter what i offered to pay! honestly superhero is the last of what you ascribed me to be. being your soulmate and best friend are what i long to be. for you to even consider me to be your personal lover and live that life with you and i am consumed in your beauty. sweetest soulmate, i am so thankful to you for bringing passion to me. to be sure there is a time and a reemerging energy and love that today I am unable to deny. i love to share with you the links that bring us back to the what was undeniable love 40 years ago. {in the olden times.} i love to write, i want you to listen and feel me. don't just listen. i want to feel your words and you. i love the wows. don't stop!

love you more

<u>romantic</u>

I am thankful i have a love of words and more wonderful is that you like them. i am blessed with the passion to share with you…. we went to a nickel arcade this afternoon. here is what you are doing to me. honest, from needing to exit for heber from orem and i have no idea how i got to pleasant grove. you fill my senses, you mesmerize my consciousness, you haunt me with such passion in the nocturne. hmmmm…i wasn't me then. i was there, i was shy struggling with esteem. you were there. you gave to me without compromise. i knew you knew one day you would grace me, recognize my hollows, overwhelm my senses, permeate my shallow veneers, measure my heart. that, then, the rhythm of two might give meaning to the drumming of one. my wish, my sweetest deb is to scratch at the surface at how you graced me then and what i feel from you today. i will always thank you. i have always loved you. i have never felt as i do today.

love you more, of course

you

you are my universe. i have heard of zumba and yoga. i walk. you are so dynamic i would join in to be close to you. there was a drought of interest and my season of words expired. i sold a bunch of books at first and i have a new publisher who is more active in promotional efforts. is there room on your couch for me to bring relief to your tired bones. i would like to try. the light and the warmth of what it was to give is your fault and it is you that is bringing me the soft caress of who i want to be for you. my mind wraps around you and me free to be in love on terms we cherish. i don't need to impress or inspire. it is only you that i care to touch with a chosen word or two. i believe there to be more words. for you, i send my love in verse. o my goodness. i need to stop. i am so yakity yak. i would love to hear your sweet voice again.

i do love you

<u>happy reading</u>

not only have you brought me out into truth and light you have
brought passion to my book. it is incredible to read and share. it
fills the pump that only pumped blood with you who i wrote it
for in 2000. you are the heart and the essence behind my sighs.
that essence is also an awakening of who we and now who we
are and will be. there is no brim to contain me. ok? promise you
will still be my most best sweetest friend as you delve into the
pages of journeys. it is me. some is rough. i know as you peruse
the love songs the light will warm you as foot jammies do and
feel as i do for you. i know the book will fill in the blanks of karl
and journeys embarked on. you hold the key. you will find me.
you will know me. you will love me more. better still you may
love me most!

happy reading my love

<u>words of love</u>

lying on our backs in the soft green of grass, passive scents drift by, earthy, musty, comfy. summer clouds invite tranquil serenity then scamper, not to be caught. shadows of carefully sculpted desires wrestle for residence on the star that was purposefully wished on and the right to be. a glimpse of the dreamyland and the fragrance of imagination give wishes life. i found sincerity in a wish on a star trusted by you and safeguarded by me. to see your sky and feel your passion, my love, for long you live and high you fly and smiles you'll give and tears you'll cry.

love you more

<u>words for you</u>

we are more than beginning, we are learning to fly. if you feel like you are falling my wings i will impart. of holidays, and yesterdays and broken dreams…..even the day comes for renewal and seeing the crescent moon as it dances through the blinds, reigns through to sheets still damp from holding to broken dreams. you are beauty, you are my light. hold the darkness and stay the night. you are wonder, you are my hearts delight. lover, are we coming home again?

coming home to you

<u>love you more</u>

to live is to reminisce in the passion of the evocative, to inhale the essence of one's sigh, then forge the union of desire and choice. capture the will, the fire of the one who lives and incendiary delights inwardly warms the soul. to choose not to live, but be only alive saves no one blinded by such folly. 'tis as a kiss on the lips of the dead. just a teardrop, you to me, and we live as well.

blessed by your teardrop

love you so much

my days, my nights, my everything, my whole me, are so mesmerized with desire, with hope, with you. charmed images take shape as a symphony of tranquility. the harmonizing of colors, as the strands of a rainbow, intertwining as two, my days, my nights, my everything, my whole me, are so mesmerized with desire, with hope, with you. charmed images take shape as a symphony of tranquility. the harmonizing of colors, as the strands of a rainbow, intertwining as two, impassioned as one, reclining impervious to anything else. coveting, your gifts find vacancy in my soul and the tenement halls breathe new life.

Yes, so much love

shower your heart

if i can bring you love, if i can shower your heart with pleasure just by holding you as your midnight love song quells the advent of a magenta sunrise ah well, my love, that's enough for me. that's all the hero i need be, we smile to think of you and me, you and i and how our closeness bestows the rarest gift ever given. no superpowers. i have attempted to capture the hero i think you would like me to be. it is what i bring to you. it is with this love i welcome you at every dawning and the life you are to my pillows as the talk of the day slips to slumber. ms. wood, that is all the hero i need be.

love you debbie

midnight love song

there is a pathway to the ethereal retreat. maybe a stage more giving than the player. shadows fill the empty spaces, vacated, now nomads of dignity lost. a single utterance on the ears of the impassioned....breath escapes with a bluster to become one with forces of creation. the awe, the rush of inhaling the grandeur draws strength, becomes the shudder, fuels the climax. words for you, so much truer than i could have never known. you and i, my love, are consumed in the hallowed hush of heaven's nearness.

love you more

afternooner

bursting to be someone and something to you, there is no measurement, no reckoning of time, just the sheer ecstasy of sharing each other. of connecting, spiraling, touching, loving the heights, challenging the angels for place among deity. serenading, the lone dancer play host to an empty ballroom. shades drawn to dim the entanglements of body and soul, yet wholesomeness fills the fulfillment of love's magic. gripping the fibers of passion, so vivid, to play to the whispers of fantasy's reality. all the while the gods weave wings of healing, pillowing, cradling.....listen.

love you more

for you my afternoon delight

the brilliant sun, obsequious, warms and soothes the bones. as if naturally, the daily climb goes on, cresting the blue horizon challenging the deep hues of the seascape, climaxing as the waning spoils of the day suspend and transform what has no equal into the magic of sunset. unparalleled shades of evening blur obscurely into an eternal curtain call. sunset, seething with majesty, vexatious with mood, suspended in atmosphere, having spent its course, relinquished the stage. warmth grows as the vibrancy of dusk reigns. the purity of true love crests as streaks of vivid corals splash the deepening twilight, splendor incarnate, breathe deeply the luster. I am taken by your love offered freely and so kindly. I bathe in that feeling with every breath, with every heartbeat and the promise of wishes wished. bring me your wishes and I bring mine to you

love you more

i love you

and in the morning of my day and in the evening of my day take me with you into your world where alone i can not go. a world billowing, swelling bursting onto a floodplain of desire. each parched receptor melting into the richness. there are stings in life's realities. rights, wrongs, the strife of choices. turn away, immerse the offense and the offender, to then savor the secret wish. run now, find the escapade, fade into the soliloquy of slumber. so is the dream state, priceless, harmless, for refuge and shelter from the tempests.

love you more

<u>love you</u>

find your way to me in the night and i will write you a song. to walk with you on a cloudy day in fields where yellow green grass grows knee high. to kiss you on a mountain top timeless and free as your flame licks at my passion, your hair breathing as a virgin breeze. as I lay safely in your arms, all i ask is for you to stay with me, love, stay with me for the night and i will never stop loving you.

I really love you more every day

i can think of nothing else

to feel such a smile. to overcome my world. aah, the splendor of this new life. so rich, so incredible, so true. eager, together we embrace this contagious enchantment. joy and bliss, natural and warm, scintillating, sparkling, defining. together as body and spirit, inhaling the grace of a pristine dawn, as slivers of early sun perforate the night, inexorable strength of one united spirit summons the rising as warmth finds affection's pathway and lengthens each stride. this sojourn nourished with discernment, new found faith and love. celestial hands bless our worthy pursuit, ethereal grace tarries at our feet. glorious destiny beckons. deepening luster enriches who we and who we are becoming. feeling blessed with the sublimation of how our sojourn feels, confidence reigns with us we may now lay us down forever and a day.

love our eternities

<u>omg</u>

a lyrical pinprick, the satiny flight of the butterfly, i yearn to feel the sounds, commiserate in the texture. must be a language of touch, pure symbols of thot, inscribed on my heartstrings for your pleasure, where origins of noise or overture of sight tingle each resonant sense. shrill intonations liberate reverberations previously inaudible. tucked away sound, fragrance, touch, await extra sensory enlightenment. sometimes a palpation, a fleeting glimpse, chased, to be lost in a vapor of apparition. worthy of the pursuit, not willing to relinquish, i search, listen, ponder phrases unsung. finally, you, my love, you are the foundation of such love, i find myself in awe, and await a hush and a wondrous the beautiful union of the two that have surpassed the needs of the one.

i love you

just a love song

compassionate, gentle wonder, these gifts you have bathed my feet in. you are the foundation of such greatness. i remain in your awe, distant for the moment. a toast to the angels, a kiss to a guardian, an expanse, without confines, lays open before me. granted tender mercies as seem fit, the glass darkly may shed a light.

Love, more than a song

<u>this is for you love</u>

a gentle soul shy tid•ar, heights unrivaled. this kiss, our first kiss, the lips that met, the splicing of time, the union. enchantment: elevating a first blessed kiss, lips wet to bring relief to a drought of touch. the sweetness as lips find the other. a kiss to stir distant memories of another time. this time to heal and give respite. euphoria: a place of dreams with no limits. the freedom of your hair tussling through my face leaving your fragrance, allowing us to soar in zealous warmth. pleasure: to release passion to each sensory receptor begging release. seeing eternity with the joining of blue eyes together again in the shade of an evening of sublime anticipation. elation: racing hearts to reflect moments of toes wrestling to keep pace as the combined breath of lovers rise to find a universe lined with fulfillment. bliss: to realize what we have always known. love is for the lovers. love is blessed with lovers without judgement, without expectation. love is for finding the amazement of the other and with a sigh, slip into the beauty of the impassioned ….

Love

love you more darlin'

incredible harmonies negotiated well before human eyes beheld the majesty. gentlest shafts of the purest sunlight bend to grace the cool of the shadows, then swells with the tide, heaving, surging, holding tight to each shimmering luminous peak, crest the curl, then break, releasing a fury of sun drenched passion. to then inhale the exhilaration of the zenith as the corals of endless sands revere each passing wave, still.

love still

just love k

there is a summons in the natural, a link inseparable. this life you and i have linked together is tranquil in twilight, yet the peace of silence is not emptiness, contrary, this blessed companionship breathes fullness to the partakers. pleasures of generations, the sandstone dawn comes breaking, rules the morn, warms the bones. the zeal of the timeless sunset also gives pleasure inimitable, belonging, untamed. life beams, brilliant, radiant, craving, being wrapped in a blanket of a supernal lullaby.

So much love

me to you....just us

the fragrance of midnight. crescent moon to split the night. night sky clings to the haze as clouds dart in and out of the moon's path. crested lips of this generous moon eager to share the soft, velvety kiss. marauding angels come to go not without giving gifts of peaceful nights, blessed dreams to surpass life's moraines, bathing hidden pain to soften in the dark of night. angels, radiant souls chase the shadows and the betrayals. heavenly ambassadors sent challenging phantoms of the dusk in the darkest of hues. cherubim light the way to scattering the dim and unholy to restoring the fervent glow and the eternal hope of the soul.

love you more

may i have this dance love

hearts confined by matters seeming without resolution, to press our flesh to the untouched, yet touchable. dreams now dreaming, emotions evade what beautiful could be, should be, beg fulfillment. faith, defining clarity, aspiring hope, and the unselfish bliss of giving takes flight in a soul's inner sanctum. so intangible to find relief. to know light obscurely left years of dancing with presumed partners to fill the measure of creation. fleeting hope, bumps and scrapes, eager, to now embrace this contagious enchantment. to the now, joy and bliss, natural and warm, defining. my sweet debbie, may i have this dance?

love you babe

omg deb

if you have nowhere left to go, stay with me. if your comforts fail you, stay with me. if your heart needs a home without deception, stay with me. love me and we span the vision of eternal sojourns together. to feel as one and break through and reconcile us to us. start a course of removing the fetters of oppressive hurt. words humbly caressed by tongues of selflessness. gazing, with hope to assuage, self to inner self, spirit to mortality worthy of replacing turmoil and the dark storms held privately. forgiveness as the falling of a lazy snow enrapture this tranquil voyage. there is no harm to accepting the gentle flakes that melt to splice love to love and heal wounds.

my love

a true afternoon delight i hope

a wispy breeze swirls through the quivering blinds singing a tattle tale song. honey, would you sing it just for me? lover, would you care to spend the night? tonight is all we have dreamed of. i know your heart in every graceful memory. i see your face in every blessed dwelling of dreams. i feel your eyes in every starry sky. so now our love of ages finds residence in every new day. now we lay us down to slumber. let me tell you a story. lay down, i know you are weary. while the stars are in the sky, while the moon is on the rise. lay down....lay down and dream of love and beauty. i say to you come unto me. you are beauty. you are light. i come unto you...

love you more

afternooner and a midnighter?

i wake at sunrise and gaze as the light swims across my room. i see the brilliant rays of a warm sun receiving the blessings of my day. i find my way across your doorway and i can't be responsible for things i do or say. words and melodies. easy words, easy melodies. symphonies of wonder. i see you walk across the same doorway, not accountable to things you do or say. jittery, giddy, even gaga elevates me knowing love to be nothing less than pure. to endure and grow, to build together. finding words, attaching melodies, easy words, easy melodies, easy lullabies defining glorious bliss. chasing the evening shadows into the nocturne, sensing the touch, breathing the close, inhaling the sublime.

i love you so Debbie

i might not let you go...

i've seen sunny days i thought would never end. i've seen lonely nights when i could not find a friend. in the glow of the sun or lost in a solitary cage my soul forever knew we would be hand in hand again. so, close your eyes and dream of me and soon i will be there to brighten your darkest nights. there are those who abuse you and those who forsake you. they will plunder your essence if you let them. don't you let them. today, imagine no regrets, no mistakes. i will never leave you, your heart will never be without mine sharing the in silky touch of love. i reminisce in your beautiful taste. i believe in us. my faith rests in us. i dose my eyes at night and i marvel where i would be without the miracle of you in my life. tender mercies beseeched, i love you

there is no letting go

love eclipses expectation

resonance permeate, betimes, and the velvet touch gives breath to wings of love. i feel the satiny flight of the butterfly, differently each time. soft pillows to cradle the weight, sleep laden eyes rhapsodize what may have forever been and what may be forevermore. life so short, beauty so fleeting. love of mine, your flame arouses my every flicker. as your flame finds solace glowing in embers eternally warm, i will clasp your hand so tight. there will always be me beside you. perhaps, defined in nearness, in flesh, in rich velour of thought, your nearness is home, tranquil.

still more love

tribute to a beautiful mother

a hopeful, humble birth, trailing peace and perfect love. he came full of savor teeming with delight. celestial hands cradled his descent to bless you, grateful mother. the travail of the mother stripped of a life born willingly, a life meant to fulfill the measure of creation. the vision to provide a finer life, to dream dreams, sweetest of parental visions. the sky is crying, the sun shyly gives light, and it's raining in my heart. where is my sunshine? where has it gone? is it a memory? where is the love i need to set me free? how can i escape this gloom that is swallowing me? may we know the hallowed hush of holding hands when i meet you at the celestial gate? i wish i could have held you one more time to ease the pain. like a shadow in the dark, like a ripple on a stream i see you float across my mind like a picture in a dream. without permission you left me but bestowed a key to unlock the heavens. the brilliance of the graceful mother finds solace in a sacred locket adorning the softness of her neck. the locket that spanned the plane of ethereal elation. the sojourn of the splendid mother arriving at the apex fusing light, life and infinity to bask in the understanding of serenity surpassing human reckoning. this resplendent mother bathes in the tears of angels to be elevated to heights known only to her. heart to heart, mother to son, life is shared through the silence of a veil of peacefulness forevermore.

i love you. i love Nathan

oh my love

oh, my love, how beautiful you are. how beautiful we are. love to touch souls, surely you touch mine. part of you pours out of me in my verse. you are a poem on a cloudy day. you are alabaster shores with palms that sway. you are the sun's heat rising without rage and the lesser light of the night that simply soothes. you are sacred music for the angels to pry loose the dead bolt to my heart's forgotten door. the passion of words felt are truly healing balms to rescue the incarcerated heart. the transparency of our souls give salvation to hearts weary of deception and life to the senses. we can make love all night til the sky catches fire, talk for hours and never tire. there is a rainbow of light about you... now you know, my love, i can no longer live without you. how beautiful you are, how beautiful we are. i love you so much...

your karl

quiet rain

though my thoughts are many miles away. they lie with you and kiss you when you start your day. the sprinkling of twilight settles as each evening ray trickles onto the bluing mist of the grandeur. the evening gives way as night sets softly with the hush of fallen leaves casting shadows on the houses through the trees. through the corridors of sleep past the shadows deep and dark my mind dances and leaps in your radiance. in the melancholy of night i wonder as the tv burns how the heart fuses with what it covets. and in the morn i watch the tiny, yet vibrant drops of a quiet rain weave their weary paths through the grates and die in the abyss. i know i am like the rain, 'there but the grace of you' go i. I, fold in your arms and your voice is the heat of the night. Fm on fire....

desire darlin'

forever dance

i love to watch you dance. as you bow your head and lift your hands. your hips begin to circle slowly. your eyes are closed, your face angelic, and hold my world as if in a trance. living in a slow dance our eyes connect, our hands softly clasp...the warmth of your breath sends shivers throughout my being. dance, angel, dance Iii you wear out your blues and with fresh light you release my affections as you do what you do. you dance in time and you move so fine like the music that surrounds you. out of the silver lining of the past you came softly calling. beautiful visions invade and we are on chadwick street once again. it is a reverent place protected by amazing grace. so, love, meet me at midnight as our love kisses the years. you cry as a lover should and sigh when it feels good. every night lying in my bed so dose if only in my dreams. if i can't have it all tonight just a taste of you if i might. i wish us strength to let love glow. i wish us strength to let love flow. i believe in angels, i believe in romance. i believe in us and our love transcending time.

i love you. i love us.

colors of sunlight

in our early days we hid our fears and passed the days alone adrift on seas of emptiness. looking back at the way we were and the hard places and chokes you never held me to blame. i remember how you comforted me, how you cloaked me in your loveliness and held my eyes in yours. i sing for you love songs. i sing them to you tenderly in moonlight and in the colors of sunlight orange and yellow. i sing to you of friends and lovers. i save for you my minutes and hours, your trinkets and flowers. i need your love, i need your light. i need your tender touch to heal my night. i see you. i see me. love is free. we are free. to see you walking by, to feel a windy sky to behold clouds reflecting in your eyes. to get lost in the softness of your skin. makes me marvel where we've been, the enchantment of forevermore together, and today....we dream, we aspire, we are....

believe

wings of creation

there is a soul in each of us looking for love. searching all we say or do or think, each reach is a reach for love. the need for words wanes and is renewed with the language of the love inside us. as the light breaks we bathe in the allure of passions unleashed. i believe in the enchantment of your every sigh. forevermore, i know of promises never broken and think of all the words between us that never needed spoken. i walk in your dream world. you give me things i could not steal if i even know what i was missing. in the middle of the night i know you, i see the flutter of your eyelids when we kiss and i adore you. i want to share in touching you and eternity. i want us to be together, so tight, to take our breath away. in the wee hours of morning i wake and i know again, the dream is real. in the arrival of the grandeur of the sunrise shining through my window i am reminded it is blessed to be alive in your love. as the sun climaxes to share light, love and warmth the day is full of promise. wings of creation unfold to brush an azure, caring sky.

i love you

i can no longer live without you

we are touched with a love that grows and flourishes inside us. you bless me with a beam of light making its way across my face. the miles that separate us disappear as i melt into you. i maybe without you but tonight, love, its only you and me. you are the essence of my every breath. you are the glow in my eyes. take me now lover as i am. you and i share desire as a hunger. it is the fire in the spirit and the banquet on which we feed. with love we slumber and i no longer can live without you. hold me tight. never before and never since, i promise, will the whole world be this warm for us to touch. in your sleepless hours you will find a hand to hold, a heart to see you through and antis where you belong. softly soar with me. let me mend your broken wings. you turn my night to day, you bring my morning sun. together we touch the moon and kiss the sky. if that sun refuses to shine and if that moon won't hang in a starless sky, if the tides refuse to change and the seasons rearrange, if the world we know is through, i will always adore you.

always

<u>more silent than a whisper</u>

you whisper to my heart without saying a word. softly i hear when you don't say a thing. the smile on my face lets you know that i love you. there is truth in your eyes saying you will never leave me. the tender strength of my hand says i will catch you when you fall. you say it best when you say nothing at all. when your heart finds you at the winds of change all that is good and true between us will remain the same. after our times of meandering along life's solitary path, so many voices, so much clutter, yours will be heard to say 'welcome home'. the stars glisten for you and just like me, they adore you. i have been looking for you since i inhaled my first breath and i will love you 'til i take my last. i dream of simple things. i believe in the day bringing the truest of love and the miracles of grace and mercy and i believe in simple things. through all our days, the blues, the grays and i believe in simple things. so, hold me close, feel my breath, lay me down, lift me up, bathe in our energy each time we touch. soul to soul, eye to eye, all our colors run into one there is no dividing line betwixt you and me...

simply adore you

more love darlin'

speak softly love and hold me firm within your essence. i feel your words and trembling moments start. our world imparts an honest love that only few have known. wine colored days warmed by the sun. deep velvet nights when we are one. speak softly love so no one hears but the heavens. together we bring serenity to a stormy sea. you understand, you give your heart. i stumbled my whole life long, always on my own. now with you i am home. home is in your arms, fears flee. the sound of your song. sing it with me forevermore. a kind of a shadow reaches into the night wandering over hills not seen. in the naked light i see gentle winds in the trees, a tranquil quiet in the air. when i stumble on my words your kiss fades my blush, that's when i love you most. pinky promises made and you can count on me for life, that's when i love you most. when the movies make you cry and you turn to safely harbor your eyes in me, that's when i love you most. nothing you do will change my mind, the more i love the more my heart overflows. that's when i love you most of

love you so much

love is at home with you

love, brilliant and fervent, rebirth beautiful. cuddled, nurtured, and benevolently caressed. love, full and brimming, gives life to sanctuaries bathed in the tears of angels, then elevated to heights known only in silent visage. beautiful souls ascended by perfect desire, purity sanctified by sacred promises we have as one. blue eyes and free hair united by tender hearts once riddled with spiritual wounds, some with intent, some heartless. no matter. healing balms don't know the difference, nor do they care, only to heal. our beautiful us, semblance of serenity, love as wholeness fills to promise renewal, pillowing, cradling, beckoning the gods to weave wings of healing. healing brushed with velvet strokes onto the canvas of the soul. a toast to the angels, a kiss to the guardians. an expanse, now enlightened, lies open before us. tender mercies beseeched, granted. to love in this chapel is tranquil in twilight, yet this silence is not emptiness, contrary, tis filled with its own companionship. gentle and guiding realms of reality dance on charmed eyelids. i know to believe in the wonders. i yearn to believe in life's miracles. life changes to open portals of spirit streaming rays of light where soul prints rest. new faith, defining charity, aspiring hope, the unselfish bliss of giving takes flight in a soul's inner sanctum in rare moments so filled to allow the world to sail by without notice. and now we lay us side by side forever and a day...

i love you. i love you renewed in spirit. i love us.

can I sing love

should i like to learn to sing? would you sing along with me? would you love to love me best of all? we sound so good together and so poorly sung alone. love, ageless and evergreen, you and i make each night the first, everyday a beginning. sip my breath on the wind. see the sky as it mirrors our colors. i grasp your ray of light. i sense your glimmer through the rain. two lights that shine as one; morning glory and midnight sun. i believe in you. you know the portals to my soul. you are my sentinel when i roam. i love you, my world is building around you. i will never leave you until my life is done. if the sky we gaze upon should tumble and fall or the mountain crumble into the sea our love will abide. pull me under, cover me with dreams. love me lip to lip, i can not resist, you are the breath that i breathe. every kiss, every touch draws me closer to your dance. the earth allows your dance, unbridled, seductive. i linger in closeness to your embrace. i hear the crystal raindrops cascade over the window to the earth below. i see it change to the morning dew as the advent of morning comes. sound, fragrance, touch sanctions the embodiment of our love, sacred and benevolent.

i will always love you....

romance me

thank you for loving me, for being my eyes when i could not see. for parting my lips when i could not breathe. i never knew i had a dream until that dream was you. as i look into your eyes the sky became a different shade of blue. i feel the color of love, it lives inside of you. i know the color of truth, it is the image of you. i found the richest love i never knew. i believe it is true, i found myself when i found you. i want to be the earth that holds you, the soothing wind that sustains you. i want to be inside your heaven. i look into my eyes and see what you mean to me. when i found you, i need search no more. you come unto me and take my hand, we dance slow, you put your lips to my ear and whisper way down low. i know you, i breathe you, i taste you, i feel you in my blood. my romance doesn't need to have a moon in the sky, my romance doesn't need a blue lagoon. my romance needs nothing but you. in this world of over rated treasures and under rated pleasures, there is you. even though you are so many miles away i will love you tomorrow as i do today, more. i am in love. i am so in love with you.

i am so in love with you...

colors of love

take me as i am. put your heart in mine forever. it is you, it is me, now it is us. two hearts drawn together bound by destiny. in your eyes i see ribbons of color. i see us inside each other. i feel your soul merge with mine. i hear a whisper say what's mine is yours. between our sheets we paint pictures, shape magic, make love. I will paint my love in shades of blue. I will paint my soul to be with you. I will sketch your lips in shaded tones. I will paint the rain that softly lands on your liberated hair. I will trace your hand to wipe my tears, draw a silhouette of holding each other in the night. I am falling into you. falling like a leaf, falling like a star, and know this dream is true. the first time, every time i kiss your lips i feel the earth whirl in my hands like the trembling heart of a captive bird. tender hearts so soft and sweet, love is the gift you give yourself. when i am feeling low, you spread your wings. when i hear no violins you play my every string. the whispers of lovers at the break of dawn rumble like thunder in your eyes. with this band of gold i do thee wed and in our lives we will never part. i offer what can not be bought. devoted love where there is no end.

i am so in love with you Debbie

my perfect you

see what i found when i wasn't looking. look what i found when i was being myself. gaze upon what i found when you found me. i need your tender touch tonight, lay it on my shoulders, lay it on my eyes. when the stars go blind and darkness floods your eyes i will carry you and we together find the way. as betimes you lose your way, close your gentle eyes, succumb to sleep, let peace invade, wake up to a fresh new day. there is magic in your eyes that makes me right. it is the light of a perfect sky it is the light of my perfect you. it is your kiss when I'm asleep. it is the love in your eyes. it is the sigh behind your blissful smile. every kiss we miss is a kiss never to be retrieved. turquoise is the sea in your eyes. emerald is the essence of a september kiss, azure is as a lonesome waterfall. crimson is the fire in your heart, for the passionate love we make as the sunset fades away. my angel, heaven starts here tonight in your arms. while i drown in our dreams, i am lost in your charms. softly now—close your eyes lightly as you fade. the moon was made for anxious lovers to keep the night away...

i am so in love with you

angelic love

stronger than any mountain cathedral, truer than any tree ever grew, deeper than any forest primeval, i am more in love with you. you bring fire in the winter, send flowers in the spring, sail through fall and summer with love on our wings. because of you my soul leaps, because of you your hand fits snug in mine. because of you my life and yours are joined. when you are not with me the hours creep like days across the ages and a year or two pass every night. our love is not a one night stand. it is written in the moonlight and painted on the stars. breathe in the majesty, breathe in the deep. the night is wild, calm and pure. hearts wrestle with each beat to heighten passion. raging lust bursts with each touch skin to skin. love is the dimming of soft lights, the scent of your hair as you twirl each lock with your fingers. the walk we share, the purity of each kiss, the honesty soothes the spirit, unveils angelic love. i watch through the mists of a dream your presence. you draw me near. you wear nothing, but you wear it so well. when in the dark loneliness of sleepless nights, know this lover, my every dream is of you. therein find peace.

thank you

<u>what love is</u>

find me... hold me...a naked heart long entombed in a crucible of vacancy bartered early for a silent pump. a fair swap, a childhood for a mask, blues of summer skies for sightless gray. wanton desertion to rule the day, tearful absence to govern the night, barely distinguishable betwixt. i beckon your gaze. i flee your probing, yearning to be found. others have been here with truth, surface intentions exposed. lies, scented, wrapped, self serving, insulting...still, a glow, so faint...i won't run. i know you, i feel your heart coursing life into mine. run to me. come for me. wait for me. fade into me. we many in this domain. i believe you. i trust you. the undoing now brings us home. restoring sight, seeing light, prevailing now in what is now a crucible of bliss your blue eyes drink me in. don't spill a drop, promise...dance in my head as i slip into your heart. now i see as you do, my eyes are blue.

i love you. thank you.

on eagles wings

i was born to love you. i love you always and forever, near and far. everywhere i will be with you, everything i will do for you. your eyes of enchanting blue melt me as we lay under the azure sky eclipsed by your resplendent eyes. feels like i stand in a timeless dream of mists of pale amber rose. feels like i am lost in a cloud deep with heavenly scents. secret moments in the heat of the afternoon unlock the stillness of soft spoken words. do you remember as we escaped the world and knew time would never find us? are we again graced by a place no one ever went before? you look inside my fantasies to make sweetest musings come true. you make me tremble as your delicate hand flits across my cheek so gently. i watch as you dance out by the sea flowing in silkiness along the sand. a spirit formed of earth, water and fire radiate from your feet. calming voices from the past join you and me building layers of harmony. melodies of life soar skyward beyond where eagles fly forever and beyond. our transcendent flight ascends through shadows of the clouds in celestial pursuit as we lay memories and dreams on the mirage of desire. angel, you were born to love me.

i love you. i adore you.

stars within our reach

i feel the magic floating in the air. i feel the sunlight wandering across my face. i have never been so swept. our dreams settle on a fragrant breeze. your words like honey settle on the essence of our slumber, slow like honey, heavy with mood. words fade into the beating of our heart. your breath rolls in over my soul. i am melting with you with nothing to prove. there is nothing i won't do to be with you. i wish you could see the way you look as you tenderly kiss my lips. it is a graceful face in sweetest of slow motion. as the world tenderly glides i fly with you, i soar with you. breathe out so i can breathe you in. you came to me out of pages of long ago, warm as the wind, soft as a kiss in a lazy snow. love is nature's way of giving reasons for living. in the morning mist two lovers kiss and the world stands still. as fingertips touch my silent heart feels like you, feels like us. your dream is a champagne toast tipsy on fields of strawberries and cream, landscapes of butterflies escaping reality, prevailing in a languid mirage. the world is small beneath barefoot dancing feet. it is when the stars above seem just out of reach. i believe we touch the stars. i believe in our dance, unbridled. i believe in our very first kiss each time we meet. i believe in debbie and karl...

i am so in love with you Debbie

you are my beautiful

i am yours in springtime when flowers bloom to wander through meadows inhaling all the sweet perfumes. at night i will hold you 'neath the nocturnal moon. in the verdant fields of summer passion and love we clasp hands in promises of forevermore. fly me high to caress the starry sky, maybe feel the astral plane, maybe chase the chill of the climes. fly me away to the brilliant side of the moon, rock me in the embrace of your adoration. no arms hold me as yours do. no heart loves me as yours does. no lips kiss me as yours do. i was made to love you, my hands to touch you, my arms to hold you, my legs, my toes in the intensity of making sacred love. my time to savor in your time, my life, your life fade into obscurity of oneness. in the cool of an autumn eve trembling hearts beat strong to each breathless kiss. a speechless hush, the tranquility of memorizing your face, i kiss you in my mind and love you all the time. i drown in your perfect, i quiver in your serenity. all i taste is the moment, all i breathe is our life. together we complete dreams softly whispered into the recesses of our soul. what you feel is what you are. what you are is beautiful.

i adore you

our immortal soul

i long to touch your soul, to taste the sacredness of you, a love so pure, sublime, serene... a dream contemptuous of time. come to me love, wrap me up in endless dreams, caress me in your sweetness with gentleness and joy. my restless heart, filled with desire would gladly soar through time and space just to dissolve in your embrace... and melt into your soul's sweet fire. you are my everything. you appear in fairest sides of deepest blue to greet a timeless morn. i dream of your lovely blue eyes swept by locks of your irreverent hair. i ldss your perfect lips and am greeted with a soft lullaby. sleep comes easy and i dream of you again. in the quiet of this heavenly dream we sit with the crescent moon, blushing. you touch my heart, you make me whole. your love, your passion move my soul. you set my spirit at ease and chase darkness away. i fancy my immortality with you. pour yourself all over me, i cherish every drop. walk this walk with me. share this journey with me. write this story with me.

i am truly so in love with you

courageous love

i know a woman with courageous love. a love that buckles my knees. a woman who knows her own heart...to you i belong. tell me how you love me. the words that touch me deeply and make my core tremble. come so close, near enough to feel all what you are to me. kiss me sweet and i crave thousands to follow. touch me as you do, let all other embrace fade into the obscurity of pale and shallow. look into my eyes, know my heart is in your hands. be gentle, my hands tingle through your hair and my love trembles at your feet. shadows of long fingers dance on the wall, flames lick the air with a silver tongue. your eyes burn bright against a frostbit world. when i am not cradled closely in your arms, i know you love me. you were meant for me, i was meant for you. i journey through your mind. i touch things you hide from, we make fear flee. love lifts us to where a cool breeze blows far above a malevolent world. i love the feel of your name on my lips. i love the sound of your sweet gentle kiss. i love how your scent lingers after you leave. i love the way your eyes dance when you laugh. i love the way you love me strong and wild, slow and easy, heart and soul. the more i live, the more i know, what is so simple is so true. i love you.

i am so in love with you, debbie...

depths of love

all through the night i stand over you. all through the night i watch over you. in the expanse of our dreams i hold your hand. when you weep you are nothing less than beautiful. you are the angel of my being. deep, deep down in your womb i am safe, i am guarded and full of life. take me, keep me. here we are, you and me, heaven is here between your lips. even in the chasm of stillness your voice permeates my essence. the sounds of silence fall lost in a dream as echoes of our mortality meet. when you say you love me, my world goes silent and still. you walk in grace as the night descends into a cloudless starry sky. dark and bright meet in your eyes ushering the tender glow of forevermore. warm as a summer's breeze, soft as a night's whisper, placid as the azure sea. the fullness of love unbound and free radiates through my heart. i recline in your tranquility content and blessed.

love you more

universe of love

love is the kiss we dream on. though all else changes, you beauty remains. how did i dwell in a world of gray? love was absent before i felt your touch. i don't know love until your kiss opened my universe. dreams take and make tales of life. never was a time when you weren't with me. you simply waited for me. at home every day you move deeper into me, inhale the same air as me. i never knew a sunrise until i woke up with you. i never saw the moon until i saw it in your eyes. i never kissed until your lips touched mine. i hear music with passion, i know the rhythm in our lusty stride. soft indulgent symphonies of thought brush with velvet strokes onto the canvas of the soul and leave hearts alive. you let me in, your trust gives me faith, you knew us, you know us still, we left the past, we soar with our future. your tender mercies greet me at heaven's gate. even waking in the same eternal sunrise all dreams are new. can love be better than this? only with every tomorrow...

love you more...

my darling

feeling you last night as you were trying not to sink i truly felt i had nothing to offer. it was the most empty place i could of conceived in the innermost passageways of my soul. today, i believe the only rational words were i was here to make you happy. for a split second there was a tear in the sky that split my night. somewhere my soul cried. all i could see was hurt and the vulnerability of the flesh. o my god...you are the strength that keeps me walking. you are the angel that gives me trust. i know the days when there was no love surrounding me. i am blessed today to be so close enough to you as to know every every breath you take every blink of your eyes, every tear... i belong to you...your love has been mine awaiting the time you would find me. i see very little less than to know this had nothing to do with our past loves, our hurt, elation or every moment we endured apart. look at my face, the years surface, lines of worry and of difficult laughter. look at my *life*. i really don't know much. what i know is the fulfilling moments of laughter you freely give sometimes out of control. I know your soul as it blesses mine with inspiration and truth. debbie, i really don't know much. i know i love you. truly, that may be all i need to know. i have never had anything less than an amazing crush on you. know your love will find a way. believe when you whisper 'i love you' in my ear i will love you forever. forever may not be long enough. why can't i breathe when we can't tell where i end and you begin? why can't i speak through times of speechlessness? why do i lose words when i talk to you? if i could speak in moments of stammering i would shout 'i love you' to the stars and the sun and the sky to permeate even where angels gracefully repose. my love, i really don't know much. the only truth i will ever know is you and me,

debbie and karl...

54

forgive and forget

i hear your thoughts. i feel your dreams. i inhale the bouquet of your skin, the savor of your kiss. the way you whisper in the shadows of dusk. my whole being is smothered by your insane, loving hair. you kindly reach every recess of my heart. i want to spend every sunset in your eyes. to stare at the night sky and drift within a moonbeam's glow. you quiet my mind, tickle my dreams and show me what love is all about. god tells me you are an angel, i already know. if i had one ticket to heaven and you didn't i would tear my ticket to shreds and go to hell with you. i muse how something as big as the earth can spin in perfect harmony on its axis while something as small as my heart can go wildly out of control. it is a marvel that both are from the same god's hand. my heart beats in your name, purest love will never fail. you are the reason i believe in love. my dreams come true because of you. never did i think there was happiness in the world and now such a unity between two mortal beings. i love you-those three words are my *life*. your voice makes me tremble inside. your smile opens my imagination to frenzy. your love to me is an endless act of forgiveness, a tender journey to forget...

love you more

love to covet

sweeter than wine, softer than autumn in new england. kisses to build our dreams on. being alone with our dreams we weave our forever romance. you fashion laughter and revel in our merriment. you intoxicate my soul through your mysterious blue eyes. i would rather be beside you in a storm than safe and warm by myself. i would rather have hard times together than to have it easy apart. i would rather have you as the one who holds my heart. slowly we begin to stir. every breath moves me deeper into you. time stands still as the dancers quench the scorching thirst. long after the glow of closeness subsides your essence remains with me, warms where your hands have touched me and my heart covets your return. your beauty speaks of love silently in a language known only to my heart. let us forever linger in our romance. true is the word of your eyes. beauty is the beating of your heart. love is the beauty of your face. desire is the touch of your hand. to wish is to wish for you. to sleep is to dream of you. to live is to wait *for* you. to smile is to think of you.

i love you forever

whisper softly

moon so bright, night so fine. it is a wondrous dream we dream. race the heavens, catch the spirit. tease the dusk to its crest. capture the iridescence. kindle the fire. embrace joy, pain subsides, watch the heavens kiss. accept my hand. dance a dance with me. your touch makes our home tender, trusting and true. images of pleasures creep slowly into your eyes so real in my daydreams. you are a hero in my heart. you have reached into my soul. any sorrow i have ever known has melted away. it's a long road when you face the world alone. you brought a breath of light, unclouded my eyes with a sweet serenity kindling hope. set me *free*. free to live, *free* to laugh, *free* to soar, *free* to shine, *free* to give, free to love. in a sea of reverie you spin in my head without end. i will think of you in my sleepless solitude tonight. i see you vividly emblazoned in my blessed dreamscape. you are away from our bed tonight. yet a distant star i see us on tonight. glittering lights, incandescent eyes silhouette your loveliness, preserve you always in my mind with unending passion, this spark never wanes. lying beside you in a blush of darkness i feel your heart in mine,

softly you whisper...

union of realms

thoughts run wild as i rhapsodize, paint a graceful picture of times we brush souls. what we have is enchanting knowing heaven has a plan. trembling knees wrapped in a warm gentle breeze. watching, an exquisite butterfly unlocks heaven's gate to drift to another time embracing happiness and the sublime. i lost my heart to you under the stars, lost in angelic <u>love. my</u> wife, my life, my everything is all in your eyes, easy, and resplendent. your sweet veneer fuels the fervor of love. when there are no words, no way to speak i hear you. when there are no tears, when there is no way to feel inside you i feel you. if the sun refused to shine, if romance fell out of rhyme, you have my heart til the end of time. you lovingly read my mind, you adoringly know what you do to me and do it. i am as a kid at school holding hands with a goddess. i know you feel me quiver, you see through me. i fly to belong in your heaven. you are the one i fly to. you cradle my glorious ascent. you cushion my vulnerable mortality. to soar with you is to let time flow and let love grow. it is to let rain shower and the rose to flower. it is the love we seek, it is the love we find. it is the love we conquer, it is the love we bind. we accept the challenge of different worlds with the love within us, there is nothing to divide us, not now, not ever.

i love you my beautiful...

true and sanctified

is romance sharing eric dapton in the night as dreams are caught. is romance moving shadows to scribe passions oldest words. spirits breathe free in the towering trees above while all my world is saying we are meant for love. romance is every note that's sung in pure love's kiss. my universe will never be the same. you have changed the way i walk. you have changed the way i talk. your love is the picture of a thousand sunsets. it is the freedom of a thousand doves. without your loves tenderness my days fade to black and white. of the times i have brought flowers i know the smile on your face. your love is a river peaceful and deep. your soul is a secret i can not keep. as i *gaze* into your generous azure eyes i know we are true and sanctified. seeing through the obscurity of my yesterdays i ponder living without the affection of your lovely face. the heart of an angel lives deep inside and leaves me purified. lost in an ethereal sigh the sands of the seas are kissed by showering mists from heaven. one long kiss and my soul escapes through your lips as the sunshine drinks the morning dew. our love is not as much to look into your face but to look together at eternity. i live in your love. you spread your love, you give your love, you share your love. i measure the serenity of our home in your love. you dreamily bestow love's true kiss and we drown in sweetest ambrosia of the gods. with you eternally mine in love there is no measure of time, you and i live in the other's heart.

i am filled with love for you

forevermore

with you warmly beside me winds of winter are infirm and impotent. with you fervently beside me roses blooms in the snow. with each passionate lts i shower you with love as you have never known. close your eyes each amorous day, trust this splendor to not recede til there is no reckoning of time. as the mounting loam carries the essence of summer, the sky is streaked with white and the soft mist of an english meadow rests calmly on our brow. we meet as lovers on this silent cliff to watch the waves bellow beneath. shall we dance on bright clouds of music? shall we soar with lofty cherubs? shall we kiss the sky? in the daybreak's virgin crest, when the last star has resigned to the sky we are drawn together in forevermore. in love with our night mysterious, in love with romance delirious it is the touching of one with another we become timeless. angels of love at our side buffer and protect us from innermost secrets. i will adore you for the rest of my... for the rest of my existence. will you be my steady girl? will you be my beautiful bride?

    i adore you

image of love

a quiet love song, a soothing serenade. when dreams come tainted with fear and pain you are my strength, you give me hope, you cradle my faith when i stumble. close your eyes, the vastness of the heavens can never elude you. this i promise. happiness is never more than a kiss away. every beat of my heart tells me i should be with you. i hear sweetest strains of harmony when i look in your eyes. i taste the rhythm of your body when it is close to mine. i feel our essence deep inside you. the way we touch saves me, your kiss, your gentle smile fills me with love. i live for this. to kiss in the sunlight and say to the sky trust in the seen and the unseen, have faith your lover adores you. i dream of you when I'm not sleeping. romance comes quiet as a sigh ushering warmth to rival the noonday sun, imparting destinies of love without bounds. in my heart there is the image of us fair and unblemished. you cover me, love resides in my heart. you lead me through the dark and through the light, caressing playful smiles, capturing tender tears. the meandering moon came escorting a lazy breeze. i touch your face, i see what you see. don't say a word, we share a heart's speechless conviction. where there is love great as ours miracles exalt our matrimonial promise.

love you baby

<u>pinkie promise</u>

when i am down and insecure you put my pieces in place, you make my universe live again. love came over me, feels right, feels pure. you know me, take my hand. on venerated ground, on a blanket of stars love settles in your blue eyes drifting like two free falling leaves on the nocturne wind. waking with the dawn i am the man who wakes up with you. gliding into the day i am the man who goes with you. on my journey home i am the man who comes home to you. peacefully growing old i am the man who grows old with you. embracing a dream i am the man dreaming of being with you. touch my tears with your kiss, touch my world with your fingertips. forever is ours today. ours is today forever. soft as a rainbow scented stardust, like moonglow i see love in your tender azure eyes. true love comes only once in a lifetime. tis now to capture our forever moment. the joy of surrendering life and soul, so gentle, so strong. you have my heart, you have my undying pinkie promise. faithful friends, immortal lovers. love came knocking at my door, i embrace you completely, my soul longs for you no more.

i adore you Debbie

<u>touch me</u>

the sun rises in your eyes. the moon and the stars are the gifts you give to what were dark and empty skies. at the end of the storm is a gilded sky greeting the sheer ecstasy of desire. moments measured, right, wrong? lay a whisper on my pillow, close your eyes and dream. look at our visceral paradise. it is the color of love. moonlight saturates our bedroom and the night is young. we hunger for love. we hunger for inflamed passion. touch me, feel me, two hearts pulse eternally. memories seep from our veins. bodies ache to breathe in the luster, intimate words unspoken make you more beautiful. a thousand angels dance with us. i dream you in my life. i see your face eyes closed embracing crystal fragrances and sandstone shores. blissfully standing on a mountain, graciously bathing in the sea, reposing forever in a place where gods weave wings of healing as stars shine brightly in a satin sky. what is a tear without a face to seek sanctuary in the heart?

i love you Debbie

never ever

close your eyes, taste this love song misting on your heart. we share an incredible place where we hide veiled in fervent love. blow out the candles, ride the evening tide. late at night when the world is sleeping i think of you. dreaming you came to me to say i love you. i love you, too. i can not wait to start my life with you. we will never be apart. i won't question the river rising. i won't doubt the open portal to the heavens. i won't turn my back to our soul's connection. i will listen to the magic of the moon. i won't hide from the sun that shines. i will listen to my heart, my soul and, yes, to the magic of the moon. i love you. i love you. i love you. i will love you until the world quits turning. love is not love unless it is with you. carve your heart in an old oak tree, hold me tight for whispered lullabies, tell me i am the man for you. every day is a new day and a new way to love you. embrace love, hold tight hand in hand. never, ever look back. let the world fall apart, we only make this heart to heart. if the world runs out of lovers we have each other. put your arm around me, never, ever let me go...

i love you

beauty grace and mercy

i dream of your face, i dream of your soft voice melting into sunrise. when the world turns indifferent embrace tenderness. in moments of silent lucidity i gently feel your voice, i compassionately hear your silence. my heart trembles as the moon sways the night and sweet tears spill into a stream of stars. rest on my shoulder when the mirror tells us we are older. i feel your beauty, your grace, your mercy grow inside me. love you give, love you live. love you make, love you take. shadows surreptitiously fall and unfold mystical charms. flesh is warm with naked feet, cherished romance permeates each moment as sweetest fantasy tarries, lusting i rest across your breast, my body in yours slipping into the night. no summer's high, no warm july, no august sky, no autumn breeze, no falling leaves, no time for birds to return to southern climes. old and new, to fill your heart, only three words will ever do. i love you.

i do love you...

flying without wings

soft and only, lost and lonely, strange as saints dancing in the deepest ocean. i rest more in love every night as you drift gently into deep, buried sleep and arouse in my dreams. you are more beautiful than music, your soothing appearance as a delicate poem and in your eyes...heaven. i have never been so close to anyone, i understand your thoughts, i reside within your passions, the fragrance of your skin, the taste of your kiss. the way you whisper in the dark, your liberal hair all around me, you surround me. you touch each place in my heart, i want to spend my life in your eyes. there is no me without you. there is no moon without you, no walk on the bluffs, no beat in my heart. we hold a powerful thing, more than three words and a band of gold. like an unbroken rhythm, like throbbing drumbeats in the night, like black coffee and honey on your tongue, i need your love. like a preacher needs pain, like faith needs doubt and lies need the dark. i need your love. so many colors surround you, some so bright i can't see. angelic light reflects on things that make you real, things that set you free. love is in the face of children. love is in your lover's eyes. when you are alive in your special love you are flying without wings.

i adore you

i do - forever

there is splendor in love resting deep inside. my soul adores you in darkness and light. love melts under blue skies eclipsing sunlight with glimmering desire. one dream, one soul, one prize. one golden glance of who we are and who we will be. the flame that burns inside sings of secret harmonies, moonlight and timeless ballads never out of date. the heavens always welcome love and lovers. hearts sweat, bodies shake, a kiss, to dream is to believe. solace is imparted on difficult days, a setting sun to warm your heart, faith to offer hope, love to complete us. every touch is new, every journey, every love songs brings me closer to you. whispering through your eyes never saying a word, your heart is safe with me. a sacred gift of heaven, for better, for worse, in sickness, in health, i do forever. love is to live bravely and prevail without fear. so many quiet walks to take, so many dreams to wake, so much love to make.

love you babe

mate of my soul

place your head against my life. what do you hear? words bursting to make love songs of an era. dreams are to speak to, hope is to call our own, thrills to press my cheek to, such love never having been conceived. spell is cast, heaven awaits us hand in hand with the universe. shadows grow long before my eyes, moving surreptitiously across the page. mystical moon looms to cloak the opaque sky as fireflies romance the greenest of trees. life was blind emotion passing without notice. you make me laugh, you make me cry, you give me wholeness. stay with me til the morning sun. dawn will be unlike what we know, all the while angels reside in our hearts. all i have known is entangled as lies, you are the simple truth. you softly touch my skin as the wings of a butterfly. i hear the beating of our hearts beneath the crystal stars knowing you share your sacred places with me. the sunlight of your smile, the seasons of our life, the magic of enlightened love, embrace the beautiful mate of my soul.

i truly adore you

poignant love songs

i want you and your beautiful face. i want you and your beautiful essence. i love you and live in your angelic grace. i know you see the heart inside of me, pleasing harmonies hum deep into the marrow. i am everything because you love me. i will be your best friend and you can be my valentine. i give you my hand knowing yours will clasp mine. you are my confidant, you are my lover. on my easel the canvas is drawn with untouched sheets of clay, to spread out before me as your body. horizons revolve around your spirit as the earth to the sun. to walk outside by a park, to crave the innocence of children, to rejoice in the laughter. my heart knows me better than i inspiring poignant heartstrings to pour into every love song. nothing is greater than the rush that comes with your embrace. tenderness, softer than velvet indelibly fuse light with eternity. dreams united sharing intensity will come true.

baby baby, baby

perfect admiration

wondrous thoughts settle on moments being wrapped up in your soul. truly loving so deeply as you have become my life and my wife. inside a magical feeling so right as to meld our essence tonight. you can't fight the moonlight, deep in the night you surrender your heart. i am profoundly proud of you, i perfectly admire you. life is full of momentous purpose with you. you inspire me to be better. to pen a love song allows heaven to permeate your heart and home. tender mercies believed and the man you married will always be the man you fell in love with. i give breath, strength, will. you give beauty, grace, mercy. i love who you are...forever. hearts of pure love shine passionately on our union. alone i dare not climb. together, we entreat at heavens threshold. to love you is to know the song in your heart, then sing it to you when you hear no melodies. your voice makes me tremble, your smile allows my imagination to run free. what is love but a single soul in two bodies.

you complete me love

love and life

show me a garden bursting with life. lay with me in the night and forget the world. sandstone dawn breaks, deep, oppressive heat greets the fiery sunrise, the majesty of the unassuming sun in noon day brilliance take me to a hillside where a stallion meets a painted sky. watching you wake i am entangled with you, in the comfort of your arms on a pillow of feathers nestled in a blanket of stars. i hear your heartbeat where i am, the heaven greet your every smile. every night together lasts forever, ends too soon. we could sit on the phone for hours and not say a word and i would cherish every minute. the whirr of the fan oscillating, the flicker of the tv playing without sound, the pleasant bouquet of your hair as i twirl it through my fingers. you lay on our bed with both hands on my waist and kiss me as you mean it, then again. if we should live forever and all our dreams come true my memories of love and life are you.

i love you forever

<u>never hold back</u>

tides rush in, cast a kiss on florescent sand, retreat to the sea, imparting peace to the shore once more. like the oncoming tide i rush to your side. hear my heartbeat whisper true, listen to how i love you. bend me and shape me, slow and sweet, calm and sleepy we won't wake the past. discreetly, there is no looking back. at first blush there is energy in the sun rays, reflecting the life dancing in your eyes. palms raise to touch the firmament, feel the warmth, live as diamonds in an azure sky. to breathe takes you in, inhales the love, drinks it deeply. the whispers you share come bathed in felicity to me. the night is wild, yet calm and serene. hearts race out of control. your gaze is smooth as you absorb my willing soul. face to face we kiss through a tender embrace, life and adoration is pure and true, we are real, we are love. in the dark, in the sun the ebb of the tide rests in webs of peaceful tranquility. there is never loss in love, the sole loss is in holding back. what we feel is who we are, who we are rests deeply in love.

meant for you love

love to love

you quiet the billowing tempest, you allow me respite, you are my promise, your hands hold me and refuse to let me fall. you are the lantern's glow guiding me to love's cherished hopes. you are the strength that keeps me walking, you are the hope that keeps me whole. you are the life to my soul. you are my aspiration, you are my universe. i taste your body when i sleep inside you. i sense your caring caress as you fulfill my desires. we kiss and touch the ethereal plane. i imagine love's kiss as i lie awake in the night. your arms are my bastion, your heart is my paradise. when i close my eyes it is you i see. your eyes give radiance to rainbow's colored ribbons. we don't love to live or to be loved, we love to love. lay your troubles on my shoulders, put your fears in my pocket, rest your love in mine. i will never close my lips to you who has opened my heart.

i love loving you

grow old along with me

dance our dance in lights soft and tender, strolling in a lazy snow to welcome the advent of spring, forgiving, graceful, warm. in the smoky haze of a cabaret a candle flickers inside touching me with your whole soul. west wind gusts under a cumulus sky, jealous sun gives way to threads of blue. your fragrant hair falls across my nakedness, touch my heart as only dreams do. visions of a lover who i know won't desert me, there is no alone anymore. the sweetest miracle is how i feel about you and how you feel about me. opposition, questions lodge at the very core. love, answers, acceptance adorn eternity with peace. as age is in my eyes and gray invades my hair, your touch immerses us in supernal care. grow old along with me, our time is now, we are one, two roses blooming in a solitary spray face the setting sun. spending our lives together, husband and wife hand in hand. grow old along with me. caught up in trivial pursuits, silent virtuous angels brought me to you...

your forever companion

a whispering world

sweeping you off your feet tonight to love deeply and keep you close, gazing captive as you spin unbridled on an old dance floor. you are the soothing descent of an angel's kiss. in love's abode there is no fear or dread, only life, love, laughter. love is what we need, love prevails in our united heart. it isn't hard to see we are in heaven catching falling stars liberating tears to cascade from your eyes. trembling hearts beat strong a breathless kiss allowing time to stand still. tenderness it isn't hard to find, it is the foundation of trust. i found a lover, i found a friend. i found comfort in promises, i found sincerity in you. a whispering world, a sigh touching the ethereal plane. love is home, heart is free, guardian angels have nothing to do but give you and me love forever true.

deeply in love with you

<u>no day but today</u>

i flourish in the shelter of your arms. i sense your sweet love and devotion deeply touching my affections. love is real, love is the miracle. your eyes shine on me, my passions unfold as your hand brushes mine. i wake to your breath, to spend my life in sweet surrender, to lose myself in this moment forever. if the world should slowly stop spinning i would spend the end with you. one by one the stars will burn out, you and i will melt away. i umbrella you when sadness fill you eyes. i could never cry your tears, but i would if i could. i loved you before i met you. you dreamed me into your life. let me surround you, my sea to your shore, my calm to your tempest. humble angels in disguise tell stories to my eyes. i love you for the rest of my life, hold you safe in my heart, know without you my soul will die. there is only us, there is only love, forget regret or life is yours to miss. no other road, no other way, no day but today.

debbie. i adore you

inside your heaven

i am your cloud in an azure sky. i am your shoulder when you weep. i hear your voice when you call. you are my angel. when you face your storm i am at your side. grace will keep us safe and warm and we will survive. when our end is drawing nigh don't give up the fight, put your trust beyond the guardians of the infinite. i am deep inside your heaven as you need a place to touch. i am the earth that holds you, every breath you take is a soothing breeze. if you were blind would you let me lead you in the darkness, in the night, in the silence? if we could bathe together high in the summer sky would you meet me at heaven's threshold? if there is madness in your head, will the sadness leave you broken in your bed? i hold you in despair's deepest abyss. dancing, spinning through angelic realms the moon cradles twilight's unveiling, sings with the wind flickering through the night. in your eyes i touch the light and feel the fervor, i am complete. stay beside me through your years, you will find happy tears, though i make mistakes, i will never break your heart. my heart will always beat your name, our love will never fail.

forever your lover

love to be loved

lay a whisper on my pillow. leave winter's chill in the clime. waking hand in hand there is passion embracing. knowing we are together i am sheltered in your heart. so many quiet walks to take, so many inspired dreams to wake, so much fiery love to make. arms to be my haven, truth that doesn't change, someone to lean on, hearts to rely on. refuge from the storm, a friend, a lover, safe and warm. strength to be strong, will to carry on all that is true. there is no sweeter gift heaven can bring than the taste of your kiss, walking in a dream to fill my head. dancing in desire, watching you spill across our bed. love floods our countenance leaving lonely days in the past, making life a blossoming love song. souls speaking through your eyes kiss through your gaze. arousing, the first sweet sleep of night ascends to where the winds breathe low and stars shine bright. live the beat, let it be your lover. liberate your mind, release your soul. watch as your inhibitions ebb into the bluster. dance to free your wings. love to be loved.

loved, always

who could love you more

i hear your voice calling my name so sweet as from the lips of an angel, words that buckle me to my knees. there are other tender voices here for you needing to be heard. the scent of magic, the beauty that is love wilder than the wind. exhale and a kiss finds me from across the room, touch my hair as you pass, take my hand when i am lost, bestow me your shoulder to brush, give your heart to love me. send the warmth of a secret smile, never forgotten, now and forever, always and ever. little things mean a lot. life, real and true is daunting to face alone, love is what we need. to look inside your eyes i am lost inside your kiss. you are like heaven to hold, like a flame when i am cold. the rays of the sun stream through the waves of your hair, every star in the sky is reflected in your eyes. in the hush of sunset, daylight surrenders to an eternal stage lit by moonlight finding you by my side. you are my life's miracle. you are everything i have done that is good. you are the reason i was born, my overwhelming happiness. when you smile at me, i cry. to save your life i would die. i live for your desires, forgetting my own, who could love you more? every breath i inhale is shared with you. you sleep inside my dreams, who could ever love you more?

only me

never good bye

you taught me to run. you taught me to fly, you freed me from me, your harmonies soothe my soul. love has been here all the time. never secret, never mystical. there is safety in this haven cradled in peaceful repose. hallowed wings of eternal love await our fluttering assent. i belong to you as you belong to me. your eyes are always a benevolent blue radiating love for me forever. the voice of your eyes is deeper than lips will ever utter. entranced on chadwick street, silently lucid, heart to heart, hand in hand. never good bye. ditching school, empty and aimless, faceless with transistor radios, refuge sought, no vacancy... no place to go. dance slow and close without touching in our age of requisite friendship. no more lonely, no more just me and no more just you. there is never alone in this sojourn, never good bye. there is no loving without you. there is no good night without your tender kiss, ever... one more day, one more time, one more sunset is never enough. trials are real, share with me, let me love you more. i give you destiny. i give you me. you give me tinder to ignite the fiery blaze of passion and ultimately seduce. you don't love me because i am angelic, i am angelic because you love me. never good bye...

always more love

take me away

something is in the air tonight, the sky is alive with burning fire. shadows of desire expose a bit of your sldn i have yet to kiss we meet there and feel the ecstasy of torrid love songs. like a river into the sea i flow unto you. should you set sail i will follow you into a shrouded mist. we can dance slow, feel bodies sway. dreamy songs offered to the constellations arouse dance enticing to the soul. the heavens grace us in our love making. humble spirits rely on strength staying intense with every word and every breath. take me away to a better day. take me away to a higher place. take me away to a secret place, take me away to a sweet escape. don't be gentle, live for the thrill. love is freed from confines release on a poet's page. and so i dream of fair romance, fanciful whims weave pretty stories wandering amidst wistful glories. my princess came to stay in the breath of a sigh to be birthed in a breeze rushing by. bluing dusk and a crescent moon kiss a starlit sky, desert squall whispers a lullaby, lets my arms intertwine with yours. love so immense, a blinding light only a soul can see. you came into my life, left footprints on my heart, leaving me never to be the same.

cuz i love you without limits

some beach

it is not far to paradise. catch the trade winds and find yourself immersed in a vivid silence. the artist's canvas bestows miracles, tied to tight neat corners. set fire to the rain, watch it pour serenity to brush your countenance. i will hold you til every doubt is quieted. you are precious as a flower growing wild, resilient and brimming with grace. you are the giver i wish to be. you are reverence shared under the covers, you are the answer to heavenly petitions. you induce the passion inspiring love songs. yours the voice i hunger for. heavenly hosts of angels bless your ascent with wings spread to impart warmth and sanctuary. let go, drift away in love's enchantment to be buried in sweet reverie. palm trees grow, warm breeze blows, eden is a place on some beach somewhere. there is a beautiful sunset burning the atmosphere on some beach somewhere. when the day seems dreary, rain soon to follow, plans made guide me your strong loving arms. tis a warm and toasty snuggle crowning a cozy haven away from life's tempests. my heart is as supple as the wind, my soul is as open as the sky.

you are my adoration

love is

love is not a word or an act. love can never be wrong. love, like
the sunrise, is perfect. love resides safely within the soul. once
found it blooms endlessly. love can choke you up and bring you
to tears. There are no dark places, no shadows, no deceptions. it
grows with trust, honor and compassion. it whispers as lovers
awaken to sighs of thunder. when phantasms that surround you
get heavy and oppressive, i can be your strength. i can be your
hope. take my spirit and my sacred vow, you have my word, you
own my heart. this quest we won united. forever is our forever.
close your eyes every loving night. share the warmth in my heart.
that warmth is you. from the deepest abyss i sink into your eyes.
breathless kisses on your soft face are my fondest moments. the
lingering scent of hope stays the night, brightens the day. you
are my dream. you are my wish. you are the prism of my
rainbow. you are my hope. you are my love and my breath. i am
licked by the lips of desire. i am humbled by your capacity to
love. may the sun bring you vigor as the moon restores you by
night. may the rain wash worries away allowing a gentle breeze
to refresh the soul may love make us perfect together.

omg

take me home

you are a love song written by the hand of god, every vessel pulses your name. you gathered pieces of me strewn on life's moraine and refreshed my mortality. your love has run into my arms, collided with my heart and exploded into my soul. fervent love splices the infinite where tranquility and warmth lives and loves. love is a forgiving, an elusive struggle to coalesce a forgetting. your tender eyes take me to depths of your soul consumed within the rhythmic beating of your heart. to love and to be loved is to face the sun from both sides. think from the mind and love from the heart. i clasp your hand at the fountain of love where you drink. every drop promising eternal passion. without love life echoes of emptiness. your smile sets the sun, your eyes move the tides. the deepest love is lucid only in silence. words are easy when the language is love. dance til the stars turn blue. hold me. lay your head low, soft and bold. lead me. guide and feed me, kiss and free me. save me. heal and bathe me. feel me and love me. take me home.

i love every day with you

tomorrows

you are a beautiful taste, an apparition of beauty and grace. daylight fades to darkness when pondering your awakening. i touch the tender lines of your sleeping body, the curve of your hip and your shoulder, the soft rounding of your breast. in the witching hour of a tropic night a careless moonbeam enchants our path. love is the season for a passionate heart to rest. i want only you to sip my quiver as you kiss me in the dark. i read the signs between us. i feel you deep inside as you come nearer. there is a stillness when there is no one else. every moment stays in the moment. in my dreams i hold your soul above the sky, in my heart. betimes, i can't believe it is you. i can't believe it is true. you call me friend... changing, our love glitters as gold. as we grow old, our love grows new. as hope seems hard to grasp i am the blue in your eyes, the twinkle in your stars. your heart is a fire burning in my soul touching me like the sun. love changes everyone, everything. nothing in our world needs be different, love remains the same. i believe, i trust and i love our tomorrows... even when today doesn't know.

it is you i love

www.ingramcontent.com/pod-product-compliance
Lightning Source LLC
Chambersburg PA
CBHW020327130626
46549CB00003B/1060